CONNECTING QUESTIONS

FOR ENGAGED
COUPLES

D1547283

CASEY & MEYGAN CASTON

COFOUNDERS OF MARRIAGE365

Copyright © 2018 by Casey and Meygan Caston

All rights reserved. No part of this book may be reproduced or transmitted in any form or by any means, electronic or mechanical, including photocopying and recording, or by any information storage and retrieval system, without permission in writing from the authors.

Illustration: Sel Thomson
Typesetting: Melanie Etemadi
Back Cover Photography: Matthieu Photography

ISBN 978-1-7324358-3-4

Published in 2018 by Casey and Meygan Caston

We dedicate this to all the couples that are willing to have the tough conversations and set the right expectations for years to come.

And to Brandon and Erica. You two have been with us in some of the worst of times and best of times. Your unwavering support, wisdom, and friendship means more than you'll ever know.

CONTENTS

Make time
to connect
each day.

INTRO-
DUCTION

Congrats on the engagement! This is such a wonderful and exciting season of your relationship. Whether you plan a small intimate wedding or a big extravaganza, you are about to enter into an amazing adventure of doing life with your best friend... and of course begin your *happily ever after*!

It's hard to deny that happily married couples are electric to be around. They walk through life with a pep in their step, laugh at ease, and carry a confidence that is contagious. These couples may not always agree on everything, but situations that create tension and conflict give them the opportunity to practice listening skills that have likely taken them years to foster. Happily married couples own their mistakes, apologize quickly, and forgive freely. Listening with empathy is the benchmark of their relationship and foundation of their marriage.

Needless to say, happily married couples embody all the benefits that marriage has to offer. Research shows these couples rank higher on the happiness scales, make more money, retire richer, raise emotionally secure children, and are known as pillars in their communities. Something tells us that relationship practice *in* the home makes for healthy relationships *outside* of the home too.

With the divorce rate currently exceeding 50%, it's clear not enough couples preparing for marriage are asking the right questions. Each day we face couples on the wrong side of that statistic or fighting to come back from the brink of becoming part of it. We're here to help you fight. We're here to prevent you from becoming another statistic by providing you with questions that will prompt and guide healthy, open dialogue between you and your future spouse as you walk into this next chapter of life together.

When we talk to couples in crisis, we start by asking them if they did premarital counseling or had a vision, plan, or strategy in place for married life *before* married life. Most did nothing. Here are some of the comments we hear in our coaching sessions:

"I never knew he/she thought this way."

"Our dating years were so easy, why is marriage so hard?"

"I was attracted to how different we were when we dated. Now it seems like we have nothing in common."

"If I'm being honest, I saw red flags when we dated, but the sex was so great I didn't want to rock the boat."

Couples caught in the flurry and emotional high of dating often enter into marriage only to discover that their spouse isn't the same person they dated. In order to maintain peace while dating, they avoid difficult conversations, preventing them from seeing each other's true selves and having all the information necessary to help them decide if marriage was the right step forward.

Some of the blame on failed marriages rests on cultural myths we believe about love. For instance - *if it's true love, then everything will work itself out!* This ideal hints at the idea that relationships should come to us naturally and with ease. It goes so far as to convince us that if our relationship requires work, there might be something wrong with one or both us.

Another myth we believe is that nothing really changes when we move from dating to marriage. Wow! That one almost took us out early in our marriage. Our dating years were so easy. The emotional rush helped both of us find the creative energy to impress each other with gestures of love. Once we got married and real life settled in, that energy dissipated leaving us bitter and resentful. What happened? Did we make a terrible mistake? Why were we so bored with our relationship? There's absolutely nothing romantic about establishing a monthly budget or determining a meal plan, but that's what is required to work as a team. I think they call it adulting ... ugh!

But the major reason that couples are not having the conversations required to help them make the best decision when choosing a partner is lack of resources. Believe us when we say that we did our research before creating this book to see what's out there. There's a lot of content that talks about preparing for marriage, but nothing that actually gets couples *talking*. If you are anything like us, we didn't know where to begin asking the right questions. Nothing like marriage prepares you for marriage, so how could we have known to ask about our expectations of sex or how to manage our families during the holidays?

That's where this book comes in. Thanks to the questions in this book and insights from a couple sprinting towards divorce by year three (that's us!), not to mention all the things we've learned from other couples along the way, now you have a tool to help you prepare for marriage in a way we wish we had. Like some of you may discover in your relationship, we had unrealistic expectations of ourselves and each other. This led to so much conflict and tension between us. Adding to that already tense dynamic, we were both stubborn and unwilling to budge, which quickly escalated our conflict to combat. We longed for peace and stability but didn't realize how much work it would take. It took countless conversations and a lot of humility to finally understand and find connection with each other.

That's what we all really mean when we pursue *happily ever after*. We want a safe place where we feel understood and truly connected with the one we love. This book doesn't talk about connection, it creates it by asking open-ended questions. When you ask open-ended questions it gives you the opportunity to draw closer by listening, validating, exploring, and discovering each other.

The #1 way to build emotional intimacy is by asking open-ended questions.

How we communicate with one another is directly tied to the *quality* of our connection. Loneliness inside of relationships is on the rise, proving that we've lost the art of asking good questions. In this day and age, it seems like most of us are far more concerned with sharing what is on our mind than listening to others. But let's take a minute to think about what defines a question. Asking a question expresses curiosity and the desire to know more. Beyond that, when you ask a question, it communicates that you are looking not just for an answer, but for connection.

HOW TO USE THIS BOOK

By Date: For each day of the year, there is one Connecting Question. Turn to the date of the year and take turns asking the question listed. You don't need to start on January 1 - any day is a great day to start.

By Topic: If there is something specific you want to discuss, pick a question by topic using the index in the back of the book (pg. 208).

By Taking Notes: We've included several blank pages in the back of the book for you to write down any notes, things that might stand out to you, or things that you want to remember for the future. You can use this book for journal prompts.

WHEN TO USE THIS BOOK

- At dinner
- In the car
- On date nights
- Over the phone
- On a coffee date
- On the couch after a long day of work
- In between all the wedding planning
- ... or really any time that works!

TIPS FOR MAKING THE MOST OF YOUR CONNECTING QUESTIONS

Limit Distractions

Make sure you silence your phones, turn off the TV, and are ready to give 100% of your time and attention to the conversation.

Watch Your Body Language

Remember that 90% of communication is nonverbal, so be aware of tone, attitude, eye contact, and body posture. Use physical touch (hold hands, touch your partner's leg, place your hand on their back) to show that you are invested in what your partner is sharing.

Don't hold back

Take this advice from married couples all around the world... don't hold back. When we dated, we withheld our true feelings and opinions because we didn't want to upset each other. Honestly, we were trying to be on our best behavior and hold back the *crazy*. This is very common but not the best way to really get to know each other on a deeper level. These questions should bring up very raw feelings and maybe even new stories you've never heard. And since there is no way that you are the exact same person, it's okay to disagree on certain topics.

The last thing you want is to hold back before you get married, only to see the real side of your partner once you're married, which might not be a good fit.

Use the Feelings Words
Listed in the back of the book (see pg. 188) are over 60 feelings words to help express yourself. Most of us use the same five emotions when we talk about experiences. It's time to expand your vocabulary! Our list will help you communicate your feelings more clearly.

Listen With Empathy
We want you to experience what a *Naked Conversation* is, meaning that you can share your thoughts while being vulnerable and messy, knowing that you won't be judged, minimized, fixed, or ignored. Listening is a major component of connecting with your partner. In the back of this book we offer sample phrases that express empathy as a guide for you (pg. 192).

Keep an Open Mind
Shocker ... your partner thinks differently than you! In order to understand each other you will need to try seeing things from your partner's perspective. This can be frustrating if your partner's line of reasoning defies all logic. Be prepared that they might say something that will surprise you or even disappoint you. Stay away from judgement and focus your energy on listening.

Don't Interrupt

Interrupting sends a variety of messages like, "I'm more important than you," "I don't have time for your opinion," "I don't really care what you think," or "What I have to say is more interesting." If you are truly listening to understand your partner, you will need a moment to process your thoughts. It may feel uncomfortable at first, but allow space for silence, giving you both time to reflect and form your thoughts.

Watch Out for Triggers

If your relationship has been on auto-pilot for a while, some of the questions will bring up underlying issues that you have either been avoiding or minimizing. Triggers are a "warning sign" that this topic needs to be worked through. How do you know if you're triggered? Your heart starts to beat faster, your cheeks get flushed, you feel anxious, angry, frustrated, or even disappointed. Take a quick time out and go for a walk, take a shower, do some yoga - anything that will restore a calm state before you come back to the conversation. If you can't work through it on your own, it is ok to seek counsel from a therapist to guide you both through it.

Use "I" Statements

Try to own your feelings by using "I" statements when communicating your feelings. "I" statements are less threatening and keep the conversation calmer. For example "I felt very confused when you shared that story," rather than "That makes no sense and it's so confusing to me."

Ask Clarifying Questions

If something your partner shares causes confusion or they are having difficulty finding the right words, use these clarifying questions:

- How did that make you feel?
- Why do you think that is?
- Can you help me understand what you're feeling here?
- What are you most concerned about?
- Could you repeat that again? I want to make sure I understand you.
- Do you have mixed feelings about this?

Don't Be Too Serious

While our questions will dig deep into core memories and topics you may have been avoiding, some of the questions are just for fun and should cause some good belly laughs. Laughter and fun are two essential components of a healthy marriage.

WE HAVE MORE CONFLICT THAN CONNECTION

Here you are. You bought this book thinking it would help you fall even more in love but as you started to go through the questions, you realized how different you both are. Maybe certain questions caused shock, frustration, or confusion. "How could he/she think that way?" "I thought we were so similar and now I'm feeling like we couldn't be more opposite." "If this is the way it's going to be, then I'm not sure this will work."

If you ran into some bumps along the way, we want you to know that you're normal! Conflict is inevitable and happens to the happiest of couples. What you want to make sure is that you learn to manage the conflict in a healthy way. If one of the questions brought up some mixed emotions, rather than avoiding it or trying to prove your point, be open-minded and talk through other options. Use the tips we gave you to listen with empathy and ask clarifying questions, so you truly understand each other's perspectives. Always make sure to pay attention to your tone and body language.

Having different views, opinions and perspectives can be

a beautiful balance, if you let it be. Finding out the areas you differ on BEFORE you get married will be helpful because you can talk through it and set the right expectations.

Remember that when you get married, you begin to shift from "my dreams" to "our dreams" and "your family traditions" to "our family traditions". This can only happen once you begin to discuss all the little details of life from how to organize the kitchen to deciding whose family to celebrate the holidays with. These are absolutely critical conversations to have before you get married. The questions in this book will spark those conversations.

A couple of tips for when you don't see eye to eye:

If the conversation gets heated, take a break and come back to it in a week. That will give you both time to proccess what feelings you're experiencing and what you want to communicate to each other.

When we are passionate about something, we don't typically consider other ideas or opinions. We view differing opinions as a threat. So take a deep breath and before you try to convince your fiancé to agree with you, listen with understanding and try to hear their heart.

Avoiding conflict might seem like a good idea but the issue will come back to the surface eventually. It might rear its ugly head in 10 days, 10 months, or even 10 years. Avoiding difficult topics brings false peace to the relationship. Be courageous and do what is right over what is easy and deal with your conflicts head on.

In marriage there is no "your way" or "my way"... it's about finding a solution that works best for both of you. Try to list out at least five other options that could be the solutions to the issue and try each one.

Ultimately, if you run into an issue that leaves you both locked in opposition to each other, find a third party to provide some insight. This would be a good time to reach out to a counselor, trusted mentor couple, or a local pastor to talk things out. Ideally, if you have to walk away from your relationship because your partner is unwilling to put the time and effort to make things work, consider that a win. Yes, it will be a heartbreaking experience, but imagine how much more difficult it will be when you are married with kids and have spent years tirelessly making efforts, feeling lonely and undervalued, and then have to go through a divorce. Trust us on this one ... consider yourself the wiser if you have to walk away before you sign that marriage license.

A great marriage is built on the foundations you lay today.

1

JANUARY

JANUARY 1

Do you have a willingness to learn more
about yourself? Why do you think that is?
What steps are you taking to become a
better person?

JANUARY 2

What is your favorite way to spend
a weekend?

JANUARY 3

When did you know you were in love with me?

JANUARY 4

What are ways we can make sure our sexual intimacy stays a priority once we are married?

JANUARY 5

How would you rank the priorities in your life: work, family, spouse, friends, hobbies, church, school, etc.? Does your ranking reflect the amount of time you spend on each?

JANUARY 6

How compatible are we in our spending habits and how will we handle finances once we are married?

JANUARY 7

What did your past relationships teach you
about love, trust, and commitment?

JANUARY 8

How much money should we spend on
entertainment each month and what would
that ideally include?

JANUARY 9

How will you make the transition from dating/
single life to married and committed?

JANUARY 10

Have I ever done anything that made you feel like you cannot share your struggles, thoughts, or ideas with me? Explain.

JANUARY 11

If I notice that you are not following through with something, what is the most effective way to let you know?

JANUARY 12

What are five things we have in common?

JANUARY 13

Why do you think pornography use is on the
rise with both men and women?
Do you think it presents a false fantasy?

JANUARY 14

Do you prefer a structured or flexible
daily schedule? Explain.

JANUARY 15

Do you think we are spiritually compatible?
Explain.

JANUARY 16

How were you taught to deal with your emotions? How were you taught to deal with the emotions of others?

JANUARY 17

What are three of your best memories with your family as a kid? What makes those memories stand out to you?

JANUARY 18

Is there anyone in your life that you are holding a grudge against? What do you hope happens with that person?

JANUARY 19

Share about a time when you felt heard and understood. What emotions did you feel?

JANUARY 20

What are three things I do that you could not live without?

JANUARY 21

What is the difference between failing and being a failure?

JANUARY 22

Do you want children in the future?
If so, how many?

JANUARY 23

Have there been times when you
were uncomfortable with the way I
behaved with the opposite sex?
If so, when and what did I do?

JANUARY 24

Is it important to you to live near your family?
Why or why not?

JANUARY 25

What role does sex play in our relationship?
Are we both comfortable with the role it plays
in our relationship?

JANUARY 26

What can I do to make you feel more
confident in our future together?

JANUARY 27

What can I do for you on the morning
of our wedding day to bring you more
peace and security?

JANUARY 28

Do you prefer that we have separate or joint
bank accounts and assets? Explain.

JANUARY 29

What are the primary issues we
continue to argue about? What steps are we
taking to resolve them?

JANUARY 30

Is there any history of sexual, emotional, or
physical abuse in your family? Tell me about it.

JANUARY 31

How can I communicate difficult
feelings I may have about you in a way
that still honors you?

Happily Ever After
isn't a fairytale,
it's a choice.

FEBRUARY 1

How do you feel about having our parents
come to live with us if the need arises?

FEBRUARY 2

Who will do the grocery shopping, cooking,
and dishes after we get married?

FEBRUARY 3

What is our biggest struggle with
communication?

FEBRUARY 4

Were any of your past relationships toxic?
Explain.

FEBRUARY 5

Are you willing to relocate for either of our
jobs? Is there anywhere you are not
willing to go?

FEBRUARY 6

At the end of the day, what can I do or say
that will make you feel the most loved?

FEBRUARY 7

Is social media bringing us closer together or making us more isolated and alone? Explain.

FEBRUARY 8

How soon after an argument are you willing to be intimate? What are your thoughts about "makeup sex"?

FEBRUARY 9

What values do you want to teach our children?

FEBRUARY 10

How often do you want to take vacations
once we are married? Are there any specific
destinations you want to visit together?

FEBRUARY 11

Do you believe there are things in life
that are unforgivable? Explain.

FEBRUARY 12

If you could make one rule that everyone
had to follow for one day, which rule
would you make?

FEBRUARY 13

Which three qualities of mine were
you first attracted to?

FEBRUARY 14

What are your expectations of how we spend
Valentine's Day once we are married?

FEBRUARY 15

Do you have any fears or concerns going
into our wedding night and honeymoon?

FEBRUARY 16

When was a time you felt
misunderstood by someone?

FEBRUARY 17

When conflict arises, do you tend to want
to fight or avoid it? Explain.

FEBRUARY 18

What is your moral compass for
making difficult decisions?

FEBRUARY 19

What did you learn from watching your
parents handle money?

FEBRUARY 20

What is one thing that I can work on to
become a better listener?

FEBRUARY 21

How do you feel when I make you a priority?

FEBRUARY 22

What are some of the highlights and lowlights
of your adolescent years?

FEBRUARY 23

If we are unable to get pregnant naturally,
would you be open to fertility treatments
such as In Vitro Fertilization (IVF), artificial
insemination, or surrogacy? Explain.

FEBRUARY 24

What should we do if one of us does not
follow through with household responsibilities?

FEBRUARY 25

How many times do you want
to be intimate each week?

FEBRUARY 26

How often would you like us to go over
our budget and finances?

FEBRUARY 27

Which of your friends, co-workers, or family
members make you feel secure and confident
about yourself?

FEBRUARY 28

Do you have a favorite adventure that we
took together? What made it your favorite?

Communicate your needs even when it's uncomfortable.

MARCH

MARCH 1

What is one failure that you have turned
into a valuable lesson?

MARCH 2

How often should we eat out each week?
Do you have specific places in mind?

MARCH 3

Are there any areas regarding sex that cause
concern or confusion? Explain.

MARCH 4

Will our children be required to do chores around the house? Do you think they should receive an allowance for those chores and if so, how much?

MARCH 5

When you don't forgive someone,
how does it affect you? How does it affect
the other person?

MARCH 6

Do you feel like we are a team when it comes
to making decisions? Why or why not?

MARCH 7

What are some things you liked and disliked
about your previous partners?

MARCH 8

What makes you really angry?
What do you do when you are really angry?

MARCH 9

What does self care look like to you? How well
do you implement self care in your life?

MARCH 10

Growing up, did you ever feel neglected by
your parents? Explain.

MARCH 11

Does prayer have a place in your
day-to-day life? Explain.

MARCH 12

What does it feel like when I admit
that I am wrong?

MARCH 13

What are your feelings about birth
control? What methods, if any, will we
use in our marriage?

MARCH 14

Do you consider yourself a saver, a spender,
or a little of both?

MARCH 15

What is your definition of commitment
inside of marriage?

MARCH 16

What was your favorite date that we ever had?
What made it special?

MARCH 17

Is there anything that keeps you from being
completely honest with me? Explain.

MARCH 18

How important are anniversaries, holidays,
and birthdays to you?

MARCH 19

How did your parents soothe you
when you were a kid?

MARCH 20

When was a time in your life where your trust
was broken and it made a big impact on you?

MARCH 21

If you did not have to work,
what would you do with your life?

MARCH 22

What do you want the next ten years
together to look like?

MARCH 23

Are there any of my friends of the opposite
sex that make you feel uncomfortable?
Why or why not?

MARCH 24

When we have children, how will you
handle any behavior or academic issues
at their school?

MARCH 25

Are there any sexual positions, activities, or ways of touching each other that you would rather not experiment with?

MARCH 26

Which external factors have gotten in the way of communication? Examples: TV is always on, phone alerts, bringing work home, wedding planning, etc.

MARCH 27

What new traditions or routines are you excited about creating in our marriage?

MARCH 28

How and when will we resolve
differences in our marriage?

MARCH 29

Have you had any health issues in your past?
Are you concerned about having any health
issues in the future?

MARCH 30

Growing up, what was the overall
tone in your home?

MARCH 31

What will happen if one of us loses a job or is laid off? What will be our plan of action?

True love is selfless.

APRIL

APRIL 1

What is a passion we share that we
can pursue together?

APRIL 2

How many times have you been in love?
Tell me about it.

APRIL 3

How can we grow in our relationship?
Be specific.

APRIL 4

What would it take for you to start saying *no* to things that are not as important to you so you can say *yes* to the things that are?

APRIL 5

Is there anything about marriage that frightens you? Tell me about it.

APRIL 6

Do you feel stress when facing financial problems? How do you deal with that stress?

APRIL 7

Are there any specific financial goals you want
in place before we have children?

APRIL 8

Once we are married, how will we let each
other know what we want sexually?

APRIL 9

Were your parents affectionate towards each
other when you were a kid? Why or why not?

APRIL 10

Do you feel affirmed by me?
How can I be more affirming?

APRIL 11

Would you ever be willing to go to marriage
counseling if I suggested it? Why or why not?

APRIL 12

Do you ever feel taken advantage of
by those you love? Explain.

APRIL 13

What will we teach our children regarding
faith and spirituality?

APRIL 14

Do you feel like a lot of the hurts in our
relationship are intentional or unintentional?
Explain.

APRIL 15

How much can each of us spend per month
without any rules and without asking for each
other's permission?

APRIL 16

Which do you think should have the final say
in decision making - logic or emotions? Why?

APRIL 17

Is there anything from your past that
might affect our sex life? Examples: sexual
abuse, molestation, early interactions with
pornography, toxic relationships, depression,
medication side effects, etc.

APRIL 18

If you could pick one year of your life to do
over, which year would it be and why?

APRIL 19

Do you feel like you can be assertive with me?
Why or why not?

APRIL 20

What is one thing that people do not
notice about you right away that
you wish they would?

APRIL 21

Have my words or actions ever made
you feel insecure? Explain.

APRIL 22

What are healthy boundaries we need to put
in place when it comes to having friends of the
opposite sex?

APRIL 23

What memories do you have of your family
having fun together?

APRIL 24

In what ways has our relationship
changed you?

APRIL 25

Do you consider watching pornography
cheating? Why or why not?

APRIL 26

Who will be the primary caregiver of our
children? You, me, or both of us? What will
that look like on a day-to-day basis?

APRIL 27

If you were given one million dollars, what
would you spend it on?

APRIL 28

Have you ever struggled with blaming others for your mistakes? Explain.

APRIL 29

What kind of house do we want to buy and how much are we willing to spend on it?

APRIL 30

Should we have a TV in our home? Which room(s) will we put a TV in? How much time should we spend watching TV?

Strive for progress, not perfection.

MAY

5

MAY 1

What is the most adventurous thing
you have ever done?

MAY 2

What triggers you during a conflict?
Examples: cussing, name calling, the silent
treatment, defensiveness, eye rolling, etc.

MAY 3

Where are three places on your body
you like to be kissed?

MAY 4

Do you keep any pictures and memorabilia
from your past relationships?
Why or why not?

MAY 5

Are you comfortable with financially
supporting me either short or long term?
Why or why not?

MAY 6

Do you believe that the roles in our family
should be filled by the person best equipped
for the job, even if it is an unconventional
arrangement? Why or why not?

MAY 7

What are two practical ways that I can
show my love for you?

MAY 8

Do you anticipate raising our children the
same way you were raised, completely
different from the way you were raised, or a
combination of both?

MAY 9

Growing up, were you aware of any feuds or
family grudges? Are there any current feuds
or grudges in your family? Explain.

MAY 10

Do you tend to meet others' needs
before your own? Explain

MAY 11

How can we make sure that divorce is
never an option for us?

MAY 12

What is one of your secret sexual fantasies?

MAY 13

How often do you use credit cards and
what do you buy with them?

MAY 14

Which areas of our relationship do we need to
talk about, even if it is uncomfortable?

MAY 15

What has been one of the biggest stress
factors in planning our wedding?
Is there anything I can do to help relieve
some of your stress?

MAY 16

What do you hope for in our first
year of marriage?

MAY 17

What are three things that bore you?

MAY 18

What are your views on church and other
religious gathering places?

MAY 19

What are the primary issues we continue to argue about? Which steps are we taking to resolve them?

MAY 20

What are our plans for our assets and debts before we get married? What will we do about them after we get married?

MAY 21

What boundaries can we agree on that will protect us from spending too much time with technology? Examples: phone, iPad, laptop, social media, videos games, etc.

MAY 22

How did your parents handle conflict
when you were a kid?

MAY 23

Do you want pets? If so, how many and what
kind of pets do you want us to have?

MAY 24

Do you want to buy a house or rent? What
does your timeline look like for that process?

MAY 25

How do you feel about scheduling sex?
Explain.

MAY 26

Do I do anything to make you feel
disrespected? Explain.

MAY 27

What is your idea of a perfect date night?

MAY 28

How do you feel about the pace of your life?
Is it too fast, too slow, or just right?

MAY 29

Growing up, did you ever feel like you
had to hide emotions? Explain.

MAY 30

Who do you believe comes first: your spouse
or your children? Explain.

MAY 31

Why do you think so many couples experience infidelity? Why do you think people cheat?

Loving well
requires
listening
well.

6

JUNE

JUNE 1

Which activities and adventures do you want
to plan for the summer?

JUNE 2

How did you begin your independent
financial life? When did you start paying
your own bills?

JUNE 3

When I am feeling angry, how can I clearly
communicate my position without becoming
defensive or attacking?

JUNE 4

Are there any thoughts or feelings that get in the way of me giving you oral sex?

JUNE 5

What is one compliment or affirmation you have received from someone other than me that made a lasting impact on your life?

JUNE 6

Could any feelings of affection or romance be revived if you met a previous significant other, even though you feel strongly committed to me?

JUNE 7

How often do you prefer to spend
quality time together?

JUNE 8

What are some boundaries that we need to
have set up regarding our exes?

JUNE 9

Is there anything in your life you feel
like you have not let go of that keeps you
from true happiness?

JUNE 10

Are you open to adoption? Explain.

JUNE 11

What should we do if we end up having mismatched sex drives?

JUNE 12

What were some of the religious values your family honored? Examples: generosity, hospitality, service, faith, justice, love, mission, etc.

JUNE 13

What are two differences we have? Do you think these differences will create a good balance or cause friction in our marriage?

JUNE 14

Do you feel comfortable seeking professional marriage counseling if needed? Explain.

JUNE 15

Which summer traditions did you experience as a kid that you want us to experience too?

JUNE 16

What do your family members say about our
relationship and us getting married?

JUNE 17

If you could be insanely talented at one thing,
which talent would you choose?

JUNE 18

When do you feel most connected to me?

JUNE 19

How will you handle a child who wants to
come into our bedroom during the night?
Will our children be allowed to sleep in our
bed and if so, until what age?

JUNE 20

What would you like to be known for both
personally and professionally?

JUNE 21

What would be a fun date night for
us this summer?

JUNE 22

Do you feel like we have enough
heart-to-heart conversations that connect
us emotionally?

JUNE 23

What are some healthy boundaries you have
put in place in your life?

JUNE 24

Do you feel like we have a good understanding
of how and when we should bring up issues in
our relationship? Why or why not?

JUNE 25

What do you think will help keep our
relationship and connection to each other
strong once we get married?

JUNE 26

What are your feelings about
guys only/girls only getaway trips?

JUNE 27

When your parents got angry, either with each
other or with you, how did it make you feel?

JUNE 28

Which of my physical qualities
are you attracted to?

JUNE 29

What unhealthy habits do we have
when we communicate? Examples: name
calling, blaming, fixing, minimizing feelings,
making judgmental statements,
eye rolling, shutting down.

JUNE 30

Have you ever run into trouble with debt? Do
you have any current debt and if so,
how much? Tell me about it.

All relationships,
no matter how good,
can be made better.

JULY 7

JULY 1

What beliefs do you have about yourself that
resulted from your childhood?

JULY 2

What are two things you can do
to reduce stress?

JULY 3

In which areas do you find it hardest
to be open and honest with me?
Why do you think that is?

JULY 4

If you could spend the next week anywhere in the world, where would you go and what would you do there?

JULY 5

Is there any kind of physical touch that I can engage in more that helps you feel loved?

JULY 6

Where in our relationship do we thrive?

JULY 7

In regards to past relationships, what would you do differently if you could do things all over again?

JULY 8

Have you ever upset someone because of a boundary you put into place? What happened?

JULY 9

What kinds of conversations leave you feeling more energized and happy? What are some of your favorite topics to discuss?

JULY 10

Other than schooling, what other types
of education do you want our children to
experience and how will we make that happen?

JULY 11

How do you define "needs" versus "wants"
when it comes to money?

JULY 12

What are the characteristics of a
trustworthy person?

JULY 13

What is your earliest memory?

JULY 14

How important is faith and spirituality to you?

JULY 15

Is connecting emotionally before
we have sex important to you?
If so, how would you like to connect?

JULY 16

If I spent a typical day in your shoes,
what would I experience?

JULY 17

Who do you know that is a good
communicator? Can you describe this person
and how you feel around him/her?

JULY 18

Do you think you will be more strict or more
soft with our kids? Who do think will be the
primary disciplinarian?

JULY 19

Do you feel like we are making enough time
for our relationship? Why or why not?

JULY 20

Which five things would you pick to take with
you if you were on a deserted island?

JULY 21

Which area of your life needs healthy
boundaries the most?

JULY 22

How do painful experiences help couples
grow closer emotionally?

JULY 23

What are some of the worst financial
decisions you have made in the past?

JULY 24

In your opinion, which qualities does a
healthy marriage have?

JULY 25

Where are two places you would like to make
love other than on our bed?

JULY 26

Who will manage future financial investments
and what could some of those investments be?

JULY 27

How did your parents discipline you
when you were a kid?

JULY 28

How can I comfort and encourage you when
you are hurt, fearful, anxious or worried?

JULY 29

Do you ever struggle with communicating
your needs in our relationship?
Why or why not?

JULY 30

Do you feel comfortable asking family and
friends for money? Why or why not?

JULY 31

Are you quick to apologize in our relationship?
Why or why not?

The little
things really
do matter.

AUGUST

AUGUST 1

What are two positive patterns and/or beliefs
that your parents taught you as a child?

AUGUST 2

Do you acknowledge and celebrate your wins,
even the small ones? Why or why not?

AUGUST 3

Were any of your past relationships physically
or emotionally abusive? Explain.

AUGUST 4

Are there any areas where you need to forgive yourself for a mistake you made?

AUGUST 5

How would you describe our communication style?

AUGUST 6

What are your thoughts on homeschool, private school, and public school for our children?

AUGUST 7

What would you like more of in
our relationship?

AUGUST 8

Are there any apps or websites that I
am currently using that make you feel
uncomfortable?

AUGUST 9

Are you comfortable with your body
and with being naked?

AUGUST 10

What issue do most people think is
black and white but you think there is
a lot of nuance to?

AUGUST 11

Which one of us will pay the bills?
Or will we share that responsibility?

AUGUST 12

What is the worst advice anyone
has ever given you?

AUGUST 13

Is there anything I need to apologize for that
has chipped away at your trust of me?

AUGUST 14

How does it feel when I talk to you and
show a lot of emotion?

AUGUST 15

How do you plan to save for large purchases
and investments? Examples: house, car,
vacations, etc.

AUGUST 16

What is your favorite way to relax
when things are hectic?

AUGUST 17

What is your philosophy of giving to a church
or other charitable organizations?

AUGUST 18

How did we make each other smile this week?

AUGUST 19

What did your upbringing teach you
about sex and intimacy?

AUGUST 20

If we get in a rough patch, how will we ensure
that we don't wait too long to get outside help
for our marriage?

AUGUST 21

How did your parents show their love for you?

AUGUST 22

How involved do you want grandparents to be
in our parenting and family life?

AUGUST 23

What are some barriers that keep us from
apologizing when we have made a mistake?
Examples: pride, shame, fear, doubt, rejection,
etc.

AUGUST 24

Do you feel that lack of money is a good
reason to not have children? Why or why not?

AUGUST 25

What topics do we deal with as a couple that we should not discuss with our parents and family members?

AUGUST 26

If you could change anything about the way you were raised, what would it be and why?

AUGUST 27

Do you consider yourself liberal, moderate, conservative, or do you reject political labels? Explain.

AUGUST 28

What are some ways we can have fun
together once we get married?

AUGUST 29

What are some romantic things I can do
throughout the day that would make you feel
turned on and desired?

AUGUST 30

What is your biggest struggle when
communicating? What is one thing you can do
today to start working on that?

AUGUST 31

What can we start doing today that will prepare us for a financial emergency?

Respect each
other with both
your words and
your actions.

SEPTEMBER 1

If you were president for the week, what is
one thing you would do or change?

SEPTEMBER 2

What do you wish you could tell
yourself five years ago?

SEPTEMBER 3

Do we effectively communicate about areas of
conflict in our relationship? Explain.

SEPTEMBER 4

Do you feel anxious about any specific body
part of yours or mine?

SEPTEMBER 5

Were there any red flags you saw in past
relationships that you ignored?
Why do you think that was?

SEPTEMBER 6

Are there any topics that are highly
emotionally charged that may require us to
get outside help with a counselor? Explain.

SEPTEMBER 7

How long would you like to wait
before having children? Why?

SEPTEMBER 8

When you think about the greatest hurt in
your life, who is the first person that comes
to mind? What thoughts or triggers come up
when you think about that person?

SEPTEMBER 9

What have we been prioritizing in place
of our relationship? Examples: wedding
planning, work, friends, social media, family,
hobbies, technology, etc.

SEPTEMBER 10

How important is it to you to have other
married couples in our life and why?

SEPTEMBER 11

What do you think happens to us once we die?

√SEPTEMBER 12

What do you like about your personality?

SEPTEMBER 13

When we travel without each other, what
boundaries do we need to have in place with
people of the opposite sex?

SEPTEMBER 14

Are you happy with your current career or
are you considering making a change?

SEPTEMBER 15

What is the difference between a sincere and
an insincere apology?

SEPTEMBER 16

When one of us is not in the mood for sex,
what should be communicated so neither of us
feels rejected?

SEPTEMBER 17

How would you rate your childhood growing
up on a scale of 1-10 (10 = amazing and 1=
terrible)? Why did you give that score?
Be specific with your reasoning.

SEPTEMBER 18

How should household chores be
divided between us? Explain.

SEPTEMBER 19

What goals do you have for our future family?

SEPTEMBER 20

At what age do you want to retire and what type of lifestyle do you want to lead in retirement?

SEPTEMBER 21

Do you feel like I try my best to understand your views, feelings and opinions? Why or why not?

SEPTEMBER 22

How can I make you feel safe and comfortable ✓
when it comes to our physical intimacy?

SEPTEMBER 23

What do you have to say *no* to in order to
accomplish your goals and desires?

SEPTEMBER 24

If we ran a business together, ✓
what would we do?

SEPTEMBER 25

What types of discipline will you implement
to correct our child's or teenager's behavior?
Were these practices you experienced or are
they new ones you developed on your own?

SEPTEMBER 26

What is something you love doing, even when
you are tired or overwhelmed? Why?

SEPTEMBER 27

What kinds of gifts do you prefer
for me to buy you for your birthday
and our anniversary?

SEPTEMBER 28

Does respect and trust have to be earned?
Explain.

SEPTEMBER 29

What are some things we can improve when it
comes to talking about our finances?

SEPTEMBER 30

What was your most memorable holiday
as a kid and why?

If you want to
have a
good partner,
be a good partner.

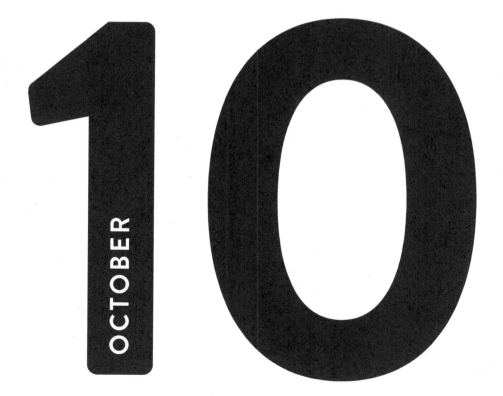

OCTOBER

10

OCTOBER 1

If your past partners listed your most negative characteristics, what would they be?

OCTOBER 2

What is your favorite thing about fall?

OCTOBER 3

Is there anything that makes you feel uncomfortable about my parents and family?

OCTOBER 4

How confident are you in your abilities to
make decisions for yourself?

OCTOBER 5

How do you feel about sexting, phone sex
and sending each other naughty pictures
throughout the day?

OCTOBER 6

What makes you feel connected
and cared for?

OCTOBER 7

When in your life have you hurt others close
to you? Have you apologized?

OCTOBER 8

Do you feel like I minimize your fears,
concerns or desires with my words or actions?
Explain.

OCTOBER 9

What are your expectations of sex
after we have kids?

OCTOBER 10

Do you think we agree on spirituality rarely,
generally, or very much? Explain.

OCTOBER 11

Who are the five people you spend
the most time with?

OCTOBER 12

Is there anything that justifies
going into debt? Explain.

OCTOBER 13

What do you think will be your favorite
part of our wedding day?

OCTOBER 14

If you could trade places with any person
right now, who would it be?

OCTOBER 15

How will we navigate a drastic career
change once we are married?

OCTOBER 16

What does a healthy married sex life
look like to you?

OCTOBER 17

What is one of the kindest things you have
ever done for someone?

OCTOBER 18

What are two negative behaviors
your parents modeled?

OCTOBER 19

Are there any people in our lives that gossip about others often? How can we protect our marriage from these people?

OCTOBER 20

Are there any areas of our relationship where we are lacking trust?

OCTOBER 21

What is the best time of day or week for us to have heart-to-heart conversations?

OCTOBER 22

Once we have kids, is it important that we live
near extended family? Why or why not?

OCTOBER 23

What characteristics do you judge
the most harshly in others?

OCTOBER 24

When I compliment you, how does
it make you feel?

OCTOBER 25

What are your family's views on race,
religion, and politics?

OCTOBER 26

What boundaries do we need to establish
with our social media use?

OCTOBER 27

If we have differences regarding our finances,
how will we plan on resolving them?

OCTOBER 28

If we eliminated physical attraction from our
relationship, what would be left?

OCTOBER 29

What is something you are
self-conscious about?

OCTOBER 30

What are the qualities of a good listener?

OCTOBER 31

What was your favorite Halloween
costume as a kid?

Create a safe place for your partner to share their dreams, ideas and concerns.

11

NOVEMBER

NOVEMBER 1

When we go to my family's house, is there anything I can do or say to make you feel comfortable and safe?

NOVEMBER 2

Growing up, how did the holiday season make you feel? Were holidays chaotic or happy?

NOVEMBER 3

What were some of the mistakes you made in past relationships?

NOVEMBER 4

How much money can we put away each
month for unexpected expenses? Examples:
medical bills, car issues, a leaky roof, etc.

NOVEMBER 5

When you are ill, how much sympathy and
attention do you need from me?

NOVEMBER 6

Which people seem to consistently break trust
in your life? What can you do about it?

NOVEMBER 7

Are you comfortable discussing our sexual
likes and dislikes? Why or why not?

NOVEMBER 8

Who would you like to be intentional about
thanking in this season of gratitude?

NOVEMBER 9

How often do you prefer us to
get together with friends?

NOVEMBER 10

Do you think you are reliable in our
relationship? Why or why not?

NOVEMBER 11

What boundaries do we need to establish to
protect our marriage from unhealthy friends
and family members?

NOVEMBER 12

What are you most excited for
this holiday season?

NOVEMBER 13

Do you feel comfortable asking for my help
or input when you feel unsure of something?
Why or why not?

NOVEMBER 14

What are ways that you would like us to
financially invest in our marriage?
Examples: date nights, vacations,
seminars, relationship books, etc.

NOVEMBER 15

How would you like to give to others
this holiday season?

NOVEMBER 16

Do you think actions speak louder than words? Why or why not?

NOVEMBER 17

What habits or additions have been passed down from previous generations in your family? How has that impacted your life? Examples: alcoholism, mental illness, addictions, divorce, adultery, etc.

NOVEMBER 18

How comfortable are you with showing affection in public?

NOVEMBER 19

Do either of us have an individual spiritual
practice? Is the practice and the time devoted
to it acceptable to each other?

NOVEMBER 20

Growing up, what were your favorite
Thanksgiving traditions?

NOVEMBER 21

In what ways do you consider
yourself to be quirky?

NOVEMBER 22

What one thing do you really want to
purchase but cannot afford?

NOVEMBER 23

Were you allowed to express your emotions
as a kid? Why or why not?

NOVEMBER 24

What budget do we need to put in place for
spending money on gifts for us and our family
members during this holiday season?

NOVEMBER 25

What was a moment when you laughed harder
than you have ever laughed?

NOVEMBER 26

Who taught you about sex?
Was it helpful or a hindrance?

NOVEMBER 27

What stresses you out most about the holiday
season? Examples: crowded stores, seeing
relatives, spending money, too many holiday
parties, pressures at work, being around a lot
of alcohol, etc.

NOVEMBER 28

What would you do with ten million dollars to
impact the most amount of people?

NOVEMBER 29

What kind of legacy do you want
our marriage to reflect?

NOVEMBER 30

Growing up, what were your favorite
Christmas traditions?

The best gift you can give your partner is your TIME.

DECEMBER 1

What goal would you like to concentrate on
before the year is over?

DECEMBER 2

What life lessons have you learned
from past relationships?

DECEMBER 3

Is it difficult to apologize when you have made
a mistake? Why or why not?

DECEMBER 4

Is there anything that stresses you out when it comes to money and managing finances?

DECEMBER 5

What is a new holiday tradition you want to start once we get married?

DECEMBER 6

What are some ways I can help you around the house? Be specific.

DECEMBER 7

What do we need to say *no* to so we can
make sure we are spending quality time
together this holiday season?

DECEMBER 8

What are your thoughts about
masturbation? Explain.

DECEMBER 9

What are some of the best financial
decisions you have made in the past?

DECEMBER 10

Are you someone who can say *no* and draw
boundaries even when it makes others angry
or uncomfortable? Why or why not?

DECEMBER 11

What are your thoughts about
prayer and meditation?

DECEMBER 12

What are three things on your bucket list?

DECEMBER 13

Do you feel like your expectations of me are realistic? Why or why not?

DECEMBER 14

How many sexual partners have you had in the past? Do you feel like these experiences will hinder or help us in our sex life together?

DECEMBER 15

Is there an argument we have had the last few months that you feel is unresolved? Explain.

DECEMBER 16

Do you want to work part-time, full-time, or be a stay-at-home parent?

DECEMBER 17

Growing up, were you ever left out, bullied or made fun of by your peers or family members? Explain.

DECEMBER 18

Did you believe in Santa Claus? For how long?

DECEMBER 19

What are your thoughts about sex toys
and enhancers? Explain.

DECEMBER 20

√What is one bad habit you need to
break but don't want to?

DECEMBER 21

√Who was your childhood hero and why?

DECEMBER 22

How would you spend your time if the electricity went out for 24 hours?

DECEMBER 23

Have you ever felt like one or both of us avoids sensitive topics? Why or why not?

DECEMBER 24

How and where will we spend Christmas Eve and Christmas Day once we are married?

DECEMBER 25

What is the best Christmas gift
you have ever received?

DECEMBER 26

What book has had the greatest
impact on your life?

DECEMBER 27

What is one thing you would like to do less of
and why? How can you make that happen?

DECEMBER 28

How do you deal with disappointment?

DECEMBER 29

Have you spent time reflecting on your past
to help you understand who you are today?
Explain.

DECEMBER 30

What do you think will be your favorite
part of our honeymoon?

DECEMBER 31

What do you think are the greatest challenges married couples face when it comes to healthy communication?

Growth comes when we face our challenges head on.

BEEN THERE, DONE THAT?

BEEN THERE, DONE THAT?

For those of you who have been previously married, these questions are for you.

Are you divorced and planning to get married again? Couples engaged to be married with a history of divorce looming over them don't have to be a victim to statistics. Divorced individuals who don't spend enough time processing, healing, learning, and growing in self-awareness drag the unhealthy habits and toxic behaviors that sabotaged their previous marriage into their next marriage. We know each divorce is unique and recognize that some of you may have gone through painful experiences caused by physical, emotional, or or psychological abuse. If this is you, we highly suggest seeking out professional couseling as part of your premarital counseling experience if you have not done so already.

With the questions provided in this book, our goal is to lead you into conversations that will prevent you from repeating the mistakes of your past relationship(s) and help guide you into open, honest - *naked* - communication with your future spouse.

Before you can enter into truly open communication with your future spouse, it is vital that you recognize and take ownership of the role you played in the failure of your marriage. Don't settle for excuses like, "I don't know," or "my ex is crazy," or "we just drifted apart." If you haven't already, this is your opportunity to do the hard work of owning your actions and calling out the habits and behaviors you want to actively work through. By starting this dialogue with your spouse now, you are setting the tone for healthy, open conversation through the course of your marriage.

Do you feel like you have had enough time to process and grow in your self-awareness since your marriage ended?

Do you think you did everything you could to make your marriage work?

What were some of the bad habits that your marriage had that you want to make sure we don't have in our marriage?

Do you have any regrets about your previous marriage? Why or why not?

Why did your previous marriage end?

What were some of the red flags you saw when you were dating that you ignored or minimized in your previous marriage?

What is something you can take responsibility for as to why your marriage ended?

Do you ever find yourself comparing our relationship to your last one?

What healthy boundaries need to be discussed in regards to your former spouse?

Do you ever feel like our relationship is a rebound from your marriage ending in divorce?

Did you do any kind of counseling to help you mourn the loss of your marriage and process the end of that relationship?

100% intimacy requires 100% Transparency.

FEELINGS
WORDS LIST

USE THIS LIST TO HELP YOU COMMUNICATE YOUR FEELINGS MORE CLEARLY

loved - romantic - appreciative - refreshed - comforted

peaceful - relieved - playful - relaxed - protected

confident - secure - positive - assertive - self-assured

happy - elated - joyful - satisfied - optimistic - delighted

excited - determined - talkative - rejuvenated

ashamed - guilty - embarrassed - stupid - exposed

sad - hopeless - unhappy - crushed - desperate

anxious - uneasy - worried - fearful - indecisive

alone - abandoned - isolated - disconnected

angry - controlled - grumpy - irritated - bitter

confused - misunderstood - deceived - skeptical

exhausted - depressed - withdrawn - lazy - beaten down

overwhelmed - burdened - guarded - tense - confused

Give empathy before giving advice.

PHRASES
THAT
EXPRESS
EMPATHY

I understand how you're feeling.

How disappointing.

That makes sense.

You must feel so helpless.

I'm on your team, babe.

That would hurt my feelings, too.

Tell me more.

I agree 100%.

I think you're right.

That would make me mad, too.

I'm on your side.

So what you're saying is...

A perfect marriage is just two imperfect people who refuse to give up on each other.

NOTES

....

....

....

....

....

....

....

....

....

....

....

....

....

....

....

....

....

....

....

....

....

....

....

....

....

....

....

....

....

....

....

....

....

....

....

....

....

....

....

The quality of your marriage depends on the level of your commitment.

INDEX

BOUNDARIES

Jan 5, 23 // **Feb** 7, 23 // **Mar** 9, 23 // **Apr** 4, 12, 22 // **May** 10, 21 // **Jun** 8, 23 // **Jul** 8, 21 // **Aug** 8, 25 // **Sep** 9, 13, 23 // **Oct** 3, 19, 26 // **Nov** 6, 11 // **Dec** 7, 10, 27

CAREER AND MONEY

Jan 6, 8, 14, 28 // **Feb** 5, 19, 26 // **Mar** 2, 14, 21 // **Apr** 6, 7, 15, 27, 29 // **May** 5, 13, 20, 24 // **Jun** 2, 30 // **Jul** 11, 23, 30 // **Aug** 11, 15, 17, 24, 31 // **Sep** 14, 20, 29 // **Oct** 12, 15, 27 // **Nov** 4, 14, 20, 22, 28 // **Dec** 4, 9, 16

CHILDHOOD AND FAMILY

Jan 17, 24, 30 // **Feb** 1, 19, 22 // **Mar** 10, 19, 30 // **Apr** 9, 23 // **May** 9, 22, 29 // **Jun** 12, 15, 16, 27 // **Jul** 1, 13, 27 // **Aug** 1, 19, 21, 22, 25, 26 // **Sep** 17, 30 // **Oct** 3, 18, 22, 25, 31 // **Nov** 1, 2, 17, 23, 24, 30 // **Dec** 17, 21, 29

COMMUNICATION

Jan 10 ,19, 31 // **Feb** 3, 16, 20 // **Mar** 17, 26 // **Apr** 19 // **May** 14 // **Jun** 22, 29 // **Jul** 3, 17, 29 // **Aug** 5, 14, 30 // **Sept** 3, 21 // **Oct** 8, 21, 30 // **Nov** 13 // **Dec** 13, 23, 31

CONFLICT AND REPAIR

Jan 11, 18, 29 // **Feb** 3, 11, 17, 24 // **Mar** 5, 12, 20, 28 // **Apr** 3, 14, 21, 28 // **May** 2, 11, 19, 26 // **Jun** 3, 9, 14, 24 // **Jul** 12, 22, 31 // **Aug** 4, 13, 23 // **Sept** 3, 6, 8, 15, 28 // **Oct** 7, 20 // **Nov** 10 // **Dec** 3, 15

FRIENDSHIP

Jan 3, 12, 26 // **Feb** 6, 13, 28 // **Mar** 6, 16, 27 // **Apr** 1, 10, 24 // **May** 7, 16, 27 // **Jun** 7, 18, 21, 25 // **Jul** 6, 19, 28 // **Aug** 7, 18, 28 // **Sept** 10, 19, 27 // **Oct** 6, 13, 24 // **Nov** 9, 29 // **Dec** 6, 30

HOLIDAY AND SEASONS

Feb 14 // **Mar** 18 // **Jun** 1, 15, 21 // **Sept** 27, 30 // **Oct** 2, 31 // **Nov** 2, 8, 12, 15, 20, 24, 27, 30 // **Dec** 1, 5, 7, 18, 24, 25

JUST FOR FUN

Jan 2, 20 // **Feb** 12 // **Mar** 21 // **Apr** 18 // **May** 1, 17 // **Jun** 17 // **Jul** 4, 20 // **Aug** 12 // **Sept** 1, 24 // **Oct** 14 // **Nov** 21, 25 // **Dec** 12, 18, 22, 26

PAST RELATIONSHIPS

Jan 7 // **Feb** 4 // **Mar** 7 // **Apr** 2 // **May** 4 // **Jun** 6, 8 // **Jul** 7 // **Aug** 3 // **Sept** 5 // **Oct** 1 // **Nov** 3 // **Dec** 2, 14

PREGNANCY AND PARENTING

Jan 22 // **Feb** 9, 23 // **Mar** 4, 24 // **Apr** 7, 13, 26 // **May** 8, 30 // **Jun** 10, 19 // **Jul** 10, 18 // **Aug** 6, 22, 24 // **Sept** 7, 25 // **Oct** 9, 22 // **Dec** 16

SELF-AWARENESS

Jan 1, 9, 14, 16, 21, 27 // **Feb** 2, 10, 18, 27 // **Mar** 1, 8, 15, 18, 22, 29 // **Apr** 3, 5, 6, 11, 16, 20, 30 // **May** 6, 15, 23, 28, 31 // **Jun** 5, 13, 20, 26 // **Jul** 2, 9, 12, 16, 21, 24 // **Aug** 2, 10, 16, 20, 27 // **Sept** 2, 12, 15, 18, 26, 28 // **Oct** 4, 11, 17, 23, 29 // **Nov** 5, 10, 16, 18, 28 // **Dec** 20, 27, 28

SEX AND INTIMACY

Jan 4, 13, 25 // **Feb** 8, 15, 25 // **Mar** 3, 13, 25 // **Apr** 8, 17, 25 // **May** 3, 12, 25 // **Jun** 4, 11, 28 // **Jul** 5, 15, 25 // **Aug** 9, 19, 29 // **Sept** 4, 16, 22 // **Oct** 5, 9, 16, 28 // **Nov** 7, 18, 26 // **Dec** 8, 14, 19

Your marriage vows are most important in the moments they are the most difficult to keep.

ABOUT HAPPILY EVER AFTER

If you have enjoyed this book and are ready to learn more about what it takes to have a great marriage, check out our self-paced online premarital course for seriously dating, engaged, and newly married couples.

Premarital courses are essential for couples entering into marriage because they help set the proper expectations to navigate through this major life change. When couples create healthy habits early on in their relationship, they will have the tools to overcome future issues in their marriage. Studies have proven that couples who go through quality premarital courses are better equipped and less likely to divorce than couples who don't.

HAPPILY EVER AFTER covers six core topics to build a strong foundation and provides a healthy start to your marriage. Each topic has its own 20-30 minute teaching video where Casey and Meygan, co-founders of Marriage365, teach and model healthy marital behaviors. Included are Connecting Question worksheets designed to get you exploring, talking, and understanding each other on a deeper level. The course also comes with action plans that will give you creative ideas on how to practically implement what you have watched and discussed into your relationship.

Learn more at **happilyeverafter.org**

USE COUPON CODE **365HEA** at checkout for $30 off

Never stop
pursuing
each other.

ABOUT
MARRIAGE365

Known as the couple least likely to succeed, Casey and Meygan faced every obstacle imaginable on their way to *happily ever after*. After bringing their marriage back from the brink of divorce, they began sharing relationship and marriage tips on social media in 2013 and quickly realized that they weren't alone. Once they realized just how many other couples were trying to figure out this thing called marriage, Casey and Meygan couldn't just sit back and watch.

Co-founding Marriage365 later that year, they have since created a variety of resources and programs for couples in every stage of their relationship. From seriously dating and newlywed couples to relationships in crisis, Marriage365 provides couples practical tools and a safe place to grow and learn how to be a better partner.

Marriage365 is a 501(c)(3) non-profit reaching millions of couples around the world each month. With a dream that one day healthy, connected married couples are the norm, their mission is to help spark that connection in others by giving couples practical tips and tools that work.

Follow @marriage365 on social media or visit marriage365.org to learn more.